SONNETS
FROM A
CELL

SONNETS FROM A CELL

BRADLEY PETERS

BRICK BOOKS

Library and Archives Canada Cataloguing in Publication
Title: Sonnets from a cell / Bradley Peters.
Names: Peters, Bradley, author.
Description: Poems. | Includes bibliographical references.
Identifiers: Canadiana (print) 20230464971 | Canadiana (ebook)
20230464998 | ISBN 9781771316132 (softcover) | ISBN 9781771316156 (PDF) |
ISBN 9781771316149 (EPUB)
Classification: LCC PS8631.E8155 S66 2023 | DDC C811/.6—DC23

We gratefully acknowledge the Canada Council for the Arts, the Government
of Canada through the Canada Book Fund, and the Ontario Arts Council for
their support of our publishing program.

Edited by Nick Thran.
Author photo by Dawson Friesen.
The book is set in Sina Nova.
Design by Natalie Olsen, Kisscut Design.
Printed and bound in Canada.

lb

BRICK BOOKS

487 King St. W.
Kingston, Ontario
K7L 2X7
www.brickbooks.ca

Though much of the work of Brick Books takes place on the ancestral lands
of the Anishinaabeg, Haudenosaunee, Huron-Wendat, and Mississaugas of
the Credit peoples, our editors, authors, and readers from many backgrounds
are situated from coast to coast to coast in Canada on the traditional and
unceded territories of over six hundred nations who have cared for Turtle
Island from time immemorial. While living and working on these lands, we
are committed to hearing and returning the rightful imaginative space to the
poetries, songs, and stories that have been untold, under-told, wrongly told,
and suppressed through colonization.

2ND PRINTING, JANUARY 2024

FOR THE IMPRISONED

CONTENTS

No one truly knows a nation until one has been inside its jails. A nation should not be judged by how it treats its highest citizens, but its lowest ones.

NELSON MANDELA

Poetry is not a tool of heroism, not a mountain from which to lecture. Instead, it's a tool of inquiry and, in particular, of failure and redemption.

MATTHEW DICKMAN

STAGE ONE

*Dependence on Institutional Structure
and Contingencies*

Mission

if prayers were   tolerable
   if money shook like rattlers
— Jordan Abel, *Injun*

Where Mustangs *Fuck You*
electronically in neon pink
above license plates fast
through blind four-ways,
where T-shirts say things
like *100% Bitch*
or *Looking for obedient wife
whom I can love and honour
and cherish* in black felt pen,
where the butcher on the strip
is content to chew the fat
for sixty years and the cobbler,
holed up in his clapboard barrack,
pre-dates asphalt, remembers

skid row for its cedars
humped down the grey clay
of James Street, the smack
of his pink gums,
his one calloused palm
charting across the shop,
over head-high shoe boxes,
shaking for age
and the rough terrain,

across Main, frosted glass
fronts, down to the river
with a splash, where spring
salmon run, where some fly
ten thousand clicks to reel

downstream, cursing
past the cottonwoods,
blackberries, around the bar,
to return broken, mumbling
a slipshod beauty,
where levees rise
to reclaim Matsqui flats,
where black bears loot
calf slunk and hipsters
reconsider backyard stashes
of scrumpy, where that burly
angel called Uncle cooks
basement voodoo juice
which the Mennonite boys slurp

in concession from the pitted ladle,
where your actual uncle lives
in a camper behind the skate park,
dickers a lift to emerge,
for the one-legged man
stole his phone, fourth
this month, where you live
in a flophouse,
where two Ziplocs

of crushed Percocets
fall divine from the closet
and the fir-plank walls
are packed with newspaper
from 1908,

where the snow-weighted
roof droops,
where a plow is for pansies,
where the coot
wheeling his bike
blind for sleet
looks like your father
smiling up, afro and glasses,
ranting *Trendy trendy*
down Second Ave,
where The Man ships inmates
of the shuttered asylum,
where officers spread hen scat
atop each ravine encampment,

where houselessness
is the new economy
of light roast beans
and warehouse pubs,
where Westminster Abbey
on the hill is besieged
with sunset virgins groping
for a sweet little plot
with a view,

where Heritage Park
is constructed
upon the rotten stone
of British Columbia's oldest
and last-closed residential school,

where plaques recount
pioneer adventures,
where garden benches
quote scripture in memory
of priests and rich donors,
where grass knolls bloom
wild rose and spring beauty,
where the cemetery
for Oblates of Mary
is fenced in gilded spires,
where the children
are silent and parents
step softly, shape the names
with their lips.

STAGE TWO

Hypervigilance, Interpersonal Distrust,
and Suspicion

Mission II

> My dear, if it is not a city, it is a prison.
> If it has a prison, it is a prison. Not a city.
> — Tongo Eisen-Martin, *Heaven Is All Goodbyes*

With fear, with rage, make yourself feel at home.
Make yourself a city inside a cell
Inside one more form of shelter. With death
There is a musk. It jacks up the senses.
COS warn about the smell at intake,
Then say strip. Death looks like an inky stain
Tainting the rec room couch. It really is
Mission Institution punching time cards
Into high school backpacks and ravine camps.
Do the dutch. Make it feel just. Make heaven
One whole apple on Tuesdays, then pawn it
Since a bible's nothing but a dream home
For shanks. Each day more men file in, each day
A guard forms a gun with his hand and fires.

Journal Fragments

Journaling appears to be well received by jail inmates, requires
minimal interaction, is time efficient, and most importantly,
may have the potential for reducing recidivism.[1]

A guard forms a gun with his hand and fires—
Just before dusk the dead come out to eat—
They get thirty minutes to stretch their legs—
Then presses it to his temple and smirks—
I am collecting fragments of the damned—
What looks like bits of bone in the soup pot—
A used shank inside a book of poems—
A milky hush of mace where skin meets form—
Memory wound scored on a plastic tray—
I feel no sense of redemption in this—
The floor buffer tossed from the second tier—
A doe and fawn at the chow hall window—
Magazines chest-strapped for body armour—
What looks like frantic birds within the haze—

Forgive Me

> The stone is a mirror which works poorly. Nothing in it but
> dimness. Your dimness or its dimness, who's to say?
> —Charles Simic, *The World Doesn't End*

What looks like frantic birds within the haze
Are really bits of brick, stones, and tear gas
Streaks above a torched Corvette as some saint,
Or could be his car, clocks two and gets dropped
By ten rights, kneels, spits blood. Sears is looted.
The Bay's windows piped out. Fifty thousand
Strong chant *Fuck the police* as riot shields
Wall down Beatty Street. Choppers, high rises
Of people who cheer, film, send full bottles
Spinning four stories, and I, forgive me,
Play my part, flip two squad cars, stomp a jig
On each exposed underbelly, and bound
Away before they get lit. Forgive me
Again, I know, I should, need to, repent.

Pleading Guilty

And eventually, when the isolated inmate's prison term expires,
our head is yanked from the sand and we are forced to confront
the creature, inevitably more anti-social, that we have created.[2]

Again, I know, I should, need to, repent
And yet I don't, and yet I kneel, and yet
The courtroom makes halos with their applause,
Which is really the state washing its hands
Of me, once more. I am set and sentenced
Beyond recognition. I walk myself
Down the aisle and I give myself away.
And yet I weep, and yet I don't, and yet
I sit and the opulent lamps shudder
Through regulation blue and red stained glass
Or is that my eyelids? In the courtroom
Guilt waits like a disappointed father
Through each revolving door. I'm a loser.
In the courtroom, I am sentenced to lose.

Scaring Myself

Half the time reach comes back
With nothing though everything
Touches everything else.
—Geoffrey G. O'Brien, *Experience in Groups*

In the courtroom, I am sentenced to lose
Twelve months, less a day, of my precious life,
Which I don't realize at that moment
Is precious—a reflection I look through
In a greyhound window, one year later,
At two buskers in the bay, one bowing
Her hot-pink violin while the other
Dozes on the bench, when, at once, my mug
Snaps into focus—I am cuffed and led
Through the side door but eke out one last glance
Over my shoulder at Grandma weeping
Into Grandpa's huge hands—and I'm surprised
When, unsure what to do, my likeness pale
In the cabin, I nod, and he nods back.

My Cousin Crawls over the Seat into the Trunk

The data also revealed a statistically significant inverse relation-
ship between pro-criminal relationships amongst young people
and being sorry for the harm caused to their victim.[3]

In the cabin, I nod, and he nods back.
"They ran the plates," he says. "Should I take off
Or stay put?" "Hide in the trunk," I tell him.
"Don't breathe. I'll pop it. When they yank me out,
Wait for a semi-truck to pass, then slip
Into the ditch and don't stop. *Look at me.*
Take the bag. Leave the bat. Dump the wallets
Somewhere but keep the credit cards, dummy."
Car doors. Boot clicks. Flashlights skirt the mirrors.
"Not a peep," I whisper. "No matter what
Shakedown or blackmail, no matter how long
In holding cells, or hunger, or photos
That place who-where then bleed out into days
And days caught between the past and nothing."

Pretend Not to Care

> Men in the Jail's GP experience psychic *dis*ease and
> an alienation from self generated by the demands of
> hypermasculine performance.[4]

And days caught between the past and nothing.
Pretend not to care. Each day postures up,
Files out like Xerox. Fight days. Pizza days.
Groundhog Day starring Hitler with a shiv
Packed up his colon in a toothbrush case.
The day two deer pass the chow hall window.
Pretend not to care. These days I don't eat,
Sleep, or shit. Days clog their guts with more days,
Then hawk ten stamps for a touch of sunlight.
When the day won't shower, shaves in the sink,
The night warns him once, then cracks his temple
Off the toilet rim. Pretend not to care.
The night shadowboxes, prays softly, chills.
Flashlights float past cell doors like blank faces.

Maybe Nights Are a Vehicle

> I lean back, as the evening darkens and comes on.
> A chicken hawk floats over, looking for home.
> I have wasted my life.
> — James Wright, *The Branch Will Not Break*

Flashlights float past cell doors like blank faces.
Jail nights: part bad dream, part white van circling
The skate park or my high school for a while
Then peeling off. Nights are creepy. Bleak nights,
I pretend prison is one lame field trip.
Some nights I stay parked. Some nights I just cruise,
First to my old street, soaked from the sprinkler,
Jeans rolled up, holding the sun-baked driveway,
Which feels like the carpet below church pews
Holding me. Congregations of dress socks
Sprint up mezzanines, skip choir, skitch bumpers
Past my young mom and old friends and dream girls.
Maybe nights are a vehicle I need
To move, get from A to B, to feel free.

The Good Guys

The very people charged with your rehabilitation are
themselves committing acts of brutality on a daily basis.
Nothing makes sense.[5]

To move, get from A to B, to feel free.
To slap on the cuffs, strip search, keep the peace.
To hammer down justice upon the domes
Of bad guys with boots and carbon batons.
To pack heat, strut down, flash a badge. To spit
Prison lingo. To get geared up, hup two,
Draw mace, pin punks, thick black vest fit just so,
Talkie-walkies, Velcro pockets that scream
Authority. To come home safe, leave work
At work, have her back, or his. To change things
From the inside. To shout lights-out and scope
Who slips into what cell with a toothbrush
Shank. To mull therapy at night in bed,
To reach out to the wife, touch her warm back.

Sponsor Me

Instead of being rooted in evidence, bans on prison masturbation seem to be primarily motivated by sex-negativity and the desire to retributively punish incarcerated people.[6]

To reach out to the wife, touch her warm back.
Skate wheels glide down alleys of smooth lamplight.
Taste the tip of her thumb raw from grip tape.
Inhale hair, exhale mute grabs and airtime.
Her tongue locks into a perfect smith grind
Down the ledge of my ear and rides off clean.
Her tongue must be sponsored. It rocks mom jeans,
Pumps fast, snakes the whole park. It inspires me.
That ass beneath a white sheet! A hill bomb
Through open intersections of green light.
I want to huck christ airs and stomp 'em bolts.
A lip bite, a hard flip. I want to work
At every sketchy trick till it's down pat.
I want to be good. I want to commit.

What I Want

all I want is a room up there
and you in it
and even the traffic halt so thick is a way
for people to rub up against each other
— Frank O'Hara, *Lunch Poems*

I want to be good. I want to commit
Passive aggressive acts on my boss, Frank.
I want to buy a pug and name it Frank
And feed him whipped cream and peanut butter
And laugh at his face, to push Frank around
In shopping carts, let him sleep in my bed,
Say *Fuck you, Frank* when he farts every night
Of his sweet life of twelve years, then lay him
By the kale and weep. I want to be sweet.
A winning smile, a firm handshake. To love
Some post of whatever. I want to dance
At church, gel my hair, belt "Amazing Grace"
Full tilt, radiate like that pantsuit mom
Down front, barefoot, spinning herself holy
Between carpeted aisles of forgiveness.

Like Home

Institutionalization as a process that includes some or all of
the following psychological adaptations: (1) dependence on
institutional structure and contingencies; (2) hypervigilance and
interpersonal distrust; (3) alienation and psychological distancing;
(4) social withdrawal and severe isolation; (5) incorporation of
exploitative norms of prison culture; (6) diminished sense of
self-worth and personal value; and (7) post-traumatic stress.[7]

Between carpeted aisles of forgiveness
Or a guard's boot heels clicking grated tiers,
I'll believe in two-thirds hard time. I'll praise
False hope like fair trials while cuffed inside
A Plexiglas box. Between men's arms draped
Through each food hatch while my pulse tabulates
Lockdown or the rift beneath resumés
And an endless dial tone, I'll worship
Bloodshot daylight, whitewalls, riots. Good god,
Your honour. My cavity is spotless.
I am strip-searched via video court.
I'll exalt the brickwork. I'll serve dead air
Shaken down and measured to a whimper
For so long that it starts to feel like home.

For This and More, I Forgive You

> I wish I could take the offspring
> out of the gnarled nests of my life
> and let them drop.
> — Bianca Stone, *Someone Else's Wedding Vows*

For so long that it starts to feel like home—
Right cross sparking off forearms and jawlines—
Gnarled fists fold themselves into rage prayers—
Eye swole shut, a warpath for gas money—
Some skinhead at point blank, some nervous town,
Bends towards me, switchblade bleeding silence
on the driveway, some whisper, and becomes
My first skid bid, flashbacks, some trembling heap.
I'm not a pacifist. I can't see how
The rain keeps its composure in a storm.
I can still see boys fighting in the parks—
One kid with black Bics as fist-fillers, one
With his skate cocked behind his head, white wheels
Moving like halos above the concrete.

Fakie No-Comply

> Look what I brought you
> It's all just graffiti
> — Michael Dickman, *Days & Days*

Moving like halos above the concrete,
My green-stained hands reek of fence tops. Spray paint
And paper bags huff into a crumple
Of nothingness then skitch down mall parkades.
Hold your shirt out and I'll put eggs in it.
Kickflip off-balance into fresh-cut grass.
Exhale and watch the night's backdrop fragment
Like a dream of broken glass through streetlight
But it's all just graffiti—*Listen—cops!*
A spotlight passes over the ravine
Almost like the hand of God. They PA
Then fade back to static, then creek babble,
Then a combo of bushwhack and stick close
To me. Stay cool, breathe. I will keep us safe.

Group Therapy Homework:
Write a Letter to Yourself

Pen-palling can provide a space for inmates to express emotions
they traditionally have to suppress to survive in prison.[8]

To me: Stay cool, breathe. I will keep us safe.
Meanwhile, doubt squats in the corner and coughs,
Then gets dressed, gets maced, gets told who to jump
And when. Stay cool. Let the current take you
Down and keep you there. The weight of it all,
Like forty-foot walls and waves of barbed wire,
Feels unbearable at first. Breathe. I will
Kill if need be. I will not absolve you.
I will resemble wolf naps and blood lines.
I will drown here. I will come back reborn.
I will, man, I mean bleed, laugh it off, bleed.
I will revive your god and learn to cry.
Meanwhile, stash shanks, stack books, fine-tune your cell
With fear, with rage. Make yourself feel at home.

STAGE THREE

Emotional Over-Control, Alienation,
and Psychological Distancing

Postcards from Inside the Machine

> Come havoc
> come mayhem   Come down
> God   and see us   Come
> — John Murillo, *Kontemporary Amerikan Poetry*

PECKERWOODS

In cuffs, willing myself clean
one pulsating streetlight
at a time while the cop swims
around me with his flashlight
cutting the fog and his face
appears pale and glistening
from the red and blue glare
like something being born.
What are you doing here?
he says and pats me down,
sighs, backsteps, blinds me.
A perfectly nice kid like you.
I'm a straight Caucasian male.
I'm white. I could be his son.

PREACH

I step into my cell ready to kill
or be killed. Officer, I too love.
Power. Respect. I share your
sense for danger. A Black man
shadowboxes in the corner
of his mind next to bibles
caught between the valley
of the shadow of death
and sizing up his new bunkie.
Shirt tucked. Sleeves rolled.
Officer, I too fear the unknown.
He glances up. *You religious, man?*
I shrug. *Well, that's something
to work on,* he says and smiles.

FISH

We all watch the dead man
walk across the unit and smile
at each table with his meal tray
like it's the first day of school.
The dead man looks lost.
He can't be more than eighteen.
The dead man sports bangles
and a bright red turban to match
the jumpsuit draped on his frame
like PJs. The dead man's dead
he just doesn't know it yet.
He grins, clears his throat, nods
at the shot callers. I reach out
to him and touch nothing but air.

TORPEDOES

The Hills Have Eyes enters my cell.
Me: You can't be in my room.
Hills: There's a Hindu on the unit.
Me: Wait. Don't come any closer.
Hills: The back table wants him gone.
Me: I said stop. Back up, man.
Hills: And you're going to bounce him.
Me: No. I'm not. Get someone else.
Hills: I said you're going to bounce him.
Me: I'm just trying to do my time.
Hills: Or I'm going to bounce
your head off this toilet.
Me: Get the fuck out of here!
The Hills Have Eyes exits my cell.

DINNER AND A SHOW

Meanwhile in Canada an inmate
with a Hitler stache raises red fists
and shouts *I'm the king of the world*
from the second tier like it's a pulpit.
Meanwhile in Canada a Stó:lō kid
returns from eighty days in the box,
wrists gnarled by chips of cinder block,
and tears all the bibles in half.
Meanwhile in Canada my bunkie, Preach,
plays aces as a sock lock blooms a pair
of red lips atop his dome and the cos
unload two cans of mace on everyone.
I fall off my chair, shield myself, and later
I stand and return to my cell unscathed.

SOCK LOCK

I sense with the knife edge of my eye
bodies shift in the chow hall, looks,
nods, and the white arc of the sock
appears like a scythe of tilting light
above your head. Forgive me, Preach.
I'm not all I hoped I was. That night
we blazed into the toilet's vacuum
and promised backup, we both knew
it was you who had to fight to survive.
You laugh across the table. I sit frozen
in the moment between grin and lock
and think maybe it won't come down,
maybe you're safe, Preach—maybe
it will just suspend above you forever.

TAKING FLIGHT

At lights-out I climb metal steps
to go fight The Hills Have Eyes.
His cell is third-last down the tier.
My shirt is tucked, my laces cinched.
I'm resolved and ready for whatever.
The CO shouts *Ten!* The lights dim.
I'm not trying to be some white hero.
Open doorways to my left radiate
Indigo and TV babble and inmates
shift in the half-light. Two OGs
cross the unit, nod and smile up
like *Go on then, Blondie.* I'm trying
to learn my place in all this. I close
my eyes for a bit—then enter his room.

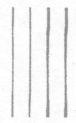

STAGE FOUR

Social Withdrawal and Isolation

Indigo

...at the roots of the mountains. I went down to the land
whose bars closed upon me forever...
— Jonah 2:6

Enter the cell and whisper *Here I am*.
This room's part echo, part flesh offering.
Dear God, are you a steel door or a key
To survive? Listen—I am still breathing
And calling it a life. I walk fear-drunk
To the same room, exact same indigo
Cage lights. They make me pace till Lord knows when—
They flicker, exhale cold air, they vibrate
Like the soul's rattle of lost hope above
Concrete altars. What light! What appetite
To absorb more and more men. Here I am,
Splayed on my bunk. Part cage, part comfort zone.
Grind me mindless with mechanical teeth.
Take me down, take me where I know the way.

Good Enough

Past behavior is generally a solid predictor of future behavior, but change (whether termed maturational reform, desistance, or redemption) is possible and frequently found in long-term follow-ups.[9]

Take me down, take me where I know the way.
Follow the clack of skate wheels. Hop the gate.
How 'bout the mall parkade with shrooms and pugs
Behind windshields pulsing like alarm clocks
Of love. How 'bout your style, that clean heelflip,
Those cream knee socks. How 'bout we gab nonsense
Then carve girls' initials in our grip tape,
Coast green through stoplights, eyes a bloom of cloud.
Let's live free from now on. Let's just mug men
Who could be our dads but not mention them,
Could be Benadryl or garage moonshine,
Then hush out into the night's damp pavement.
I turn to you but can't say it (love, fear).
Good enough to just feel you there with me.

Sleep Paralysis

But it's her he holds in his sleep, dreams in his hands, Prairie,
his knee, his shoulder, his hands in her hair.
— Nora Gould, *I see my love more clearly from a distance*

Good enough to just feel you there with me.
In bed strung out on bitter dips of X
You sleep all day say hold me and don't talk
Beneath lust beneath divorce and the moon
Is a flashlight through the slot every hour
Clinking like thirty pieces of silver
Is guilt is a flush of birds is my love
Like fields seen more clearly from a distance
I am not ashamed of how much we lost
Or how desperate like a child clutching wind
I watch you walk across my cell and think
My cell you are walking across my cell
Cool earth pressing through the plastic mattress
Beneath cage lights beneath one more daybreak

The Red Scorpions

They harass you or they stalk…and if you can't hold your own,
they'll take from you… Hardly anybody [is] solo in there…
Being solo, you're with nobody. So, if something happens,
you're by yourself against everybody.
— Inmate, Chris[10]

Beneath cage lights, beneath one more daybreak,
All clocks buzz go-time for the red parade
Of men in the war room with suitcases
full of newspaper shanks and fear. The fear
Comes packed in small balloons and is pricey.
Red Scorpions along the back table
Keep humans nearby to wipe the fear off
Their pincers while they cut it for resale.
Torpedoes load up on pure stuff then blitz
Around the war room with their eyes clamped shut
Which amuses everyone. Things get done.
Days go by. Outside, it's the first of spring.
Crack a window, I say. Let in some air.
Work to live, you rat bastards! Work to live!

Ding-Wing

Mental health observation placements, for example, typically
involve, among other measures, mandatory strip search, issuance
of anti-suicide garments, removal of personal items, constant
direct observation (via closed-circuit television, staff or both),
limited association and restricted access to showers, visits and
phone calls.[11]

Work to live, you rat bastards! Work to live!
Maybe you have to be there to hear it.
The moans. The high-pitched screams. One man wailing
There is shit everywhere! Boot clicks. Leg cuffs.
The mindless hours I lie on my steel bunk
With no pillow staring at the blue bulb
In the cinder block room, a young poet
Losing most of my hair. Ain't right. Bam-bam.
Chatted out. Ding-wing. Flipped a lid. Gonzo.
J-bug loonie. Monkey mouth. Netted up.
Psych camp. Red tag. Sleep on steel. Turtle suit.
Under watch. Vampire. Wobble head. x-Cat.
Give me more time. Take the clocks. Leave the light
On all damn night. I need to get this out.

Daydreaming in the Shower before Lights-Out

> …ten more minutes, okay? A poem is
> a way of dreaming after what
> I want and can't have I don't even
> know how this thing got here we inherited
> — Sheryda Warrener, *Floating Is Everything*

On all damn night. I need to get this out.
In White Rock after the divorce. Smoking
Again. A woman laughs in a sage dress.
Wind holds the drapes out like a dream and sounds
Wash themselves down with lime wedge and more sound.
Why do I return to these same four walls?
To feel free, to let loose. Moonwalk, high kick.
Now who's on all damn night! Not lost, but twice
I appear on wet sideroads smiling up—
A seagull arcs overhead like floating
is everything—I jog the tide to sea,
I stand drenched from the bath in cool static.
A sonnet is not memory. More so
It is a room the shape of my own face.

A Visit to the Box

While leaving the body merely singed, the torture of prolonged isolation scorches some capacity within the mind or soul to empathize with fellow human beings.[2]

It is a room the shape of my own face.
The room is heaped with jumpsuits and bobos.
Two guards laugh, stare, yell *Strip* through tempered glass.
The real room is inside another room.
Its steel door snaps shut like a mouth. It reeks
Of bleach. The room with no windows is scrubbed
Skull white. I am a tongue stuck in its jaw.
I thrash and bark nonsense. The room makes me
feral, cry fam, skip chow, crave blood. I pace
And pace. I need to try to love myself
but the room won't allow it. It dilates
Into one rage box. The room moves through me.
I stretch each fibrous limb. I bare white teeth.
My skin shines. I am clean and out to kill.

After My Daily Twenty-Minute Shower Break

> It is only a matter of time, if you love life too much or fear
> violence too much, before you become a thing, no longer a man.
> — Jack Henry Abbott, *In the Belly of the Beast: Letters from Prison*

My skin shines. I am clean and out to kill.
I am the last rainfall in September.
It's almost midnight and I am spreading
Into fine mist. I'm low-key romantic.
I love the sounds of life within a storm.
A door, a man laughing, a newspaper
Held above his head. I can lose my cool,
Lash out, clear up on a dime. The flash flood
As much as the rainbow. Bits of blue sky
The day of the miscarriage, two lovers
Groping for the words, a moment of grace
Between the lightning and its violence.
An immense solitude, a touch of wind.
The surf, the pier, the river darkening.

Learning to Live

Silence taunts: a dare. Everything that disappears
Disappears as if returning somewhere.
— Tracy K. Smith, *Life on Mars*

The surf, the pier, the river darkening.
Red bell-buoys lashed to timber pilings
Chime softly. Rain hung up like a lost thought.
A fisherman hoses down his boat deck
With a smoke in his mouth. The tiny flame
Of a beach fire dissolves across the mist.
I want to learn to live. Seagulls gust up
Like paper scraps alongside Mission Bridge
Long before I am born then long after,
Storm light glinting off wings and everything
Made up of water and stardust. I want
While the cottonwoods laugh into the wind.
A car starts. Cicadas vibrate themselves.
I stand there in the humid air and breathe.

On Quiet Nights You Can Hear Trains Down the Hill from Mission Institution

> The last assembly instruction is always you reading this.
> A machine that rarely functions but could never
> without you.
> — Raoul Fernandes, *Transmitter and Receiver*

You stand there in the humid air and breathe.
It's dark. The train grinds into the station
And you're down in the boiler room. Outside,
Endless boxcars, one caboose. You are strong,
Physically. You like the long way, weight
Straining your broad shoulders, the stomp of spade,
Steel rasp. You like to take your time, to brake
Mid track and survey angles in the slope,
Shift, restrap the load. You like your shirt off.
You like sweat beads through dust. You like to wash
With the hose real careless, hoot and shout *God
Damn* and *Oh baby!* Sometimes you're lucky
In love. Sometimes you feel weak. You sleep in,
Get blue, go mute, turn back, but you like that.

Daydreaming in the Shower before Lights-Out II

> Come nearer   there is no emptiness
> Yes it's bitter   every bit of it bitter
> — C.D. Wright, *One Big Self: An Investigation*

Get blue, go mute, turn back, but you like that.
But also, humid and feels like a dream.
This shower could be anywhere maybe.
Loudspeaker buzz really a lawn mower,
A pollen swarm, a wave-spray boardwalk view
Of the Pacific. Two dragonflies fuse
Mid-air. Seagulls. My wife down the beach. Oh!
Her thighs! Two white flags. I will carry them
Across enemy lines and surrender.
I'll tell them what they want to hear, whisper
I did it. I drew out the dark kingdom
Of the dead. I laughed and rocked my own raft
Till it flipped. Lights-out is called. The showers
Stop. I dry and dress and walk to my cell.

Back to School

Schools use law enforcement tactics including random sweeps, searches of students, drug tests, and interrogations, and they increasingly rely on sworn police officers to patrol their hallways. As a result, a growing number of youth are being arrested and processed through courts for misconduct at school.[12]

Stop. I dry and dress and walk to my cell
Single file. Must be the first day of school.
Must-have high-tops and shoelace belt, skateboard
Against the wall. Turn forward. Now headcount.
Now loudspeakers love me. They sigh my name.
I recite raps for them, like fuck homeroom
To the moon and back. Like, science is dope.
Bunsen burners and tinfoil and weed smoke
In toilet stalls. Forget gold stars. I hate
And hate, duck out, key cars. My lean frame aches
To fist fight—but also love, delinquent
Puberty blurring each lunch break—then folds
And folds outside the principal's office.
I sob. I pray. I don't want to be bad.

Back to Church

Penitentiary: early 15c., penitenciarie, "place of punishment for offenses against the church," from Medieval Latin *penitentiaria*, from fem. of *penitentiariu* (adj.) "of penance," from Latin *paenitentia* "penitence."

I sob. I pray. I don't want to be bad.
I'm the wild apple tree behind the church
Lifting bloodshot eyes to heaven. Really,
I'm on the loose, under pews, scavenging
Coat pockets and dim offices. Oh Lord,
I'm not angry! In darkness I can see,
Or begin to, a slit of dusted light
Below the stage curtain, doubt, fear, and through
To Mennonites in the choir hall singing
Thou shall oppose the serpent. Dear God, I'm
Here. I outstretch each branch heavy with fruit
Like a wound. Really, I lay myself down
Backstage and feel a great static, chants, stomps,
A chorus of men mimicking angels.

The Day My Hair Starts to Fall Out in Clumps

> Solitary confinement is a violence so radical that it could
> even alter the ontology of a stone.[13]

A chorus of men mimicking angels—
We barbarian preachers doze in stalls—
Sleepless but this is a private restroom—
Steel toilets upstream clear their throats all night—
At forty days the cage light is a mouth—
A feast of jabs naked door-kick madness—
An attempted ascension suspended—
We sing our loved ones to take us back home—
One dead-tired inmate melts into a shriek—
One day I just started punching myself—
Now it's paper gowns and daily searches—
This big hush must be the voice of lost time—
Cell doors fold into formative symbols—
Back home back home before the year is out—

The Season of Unease

If you think a hammer is the only way to hammer
A nail, you ain't thought of the nail correctly.
— Terrance Hayes, *American Sonnets for My Past and Future Assassin*

Back home, back home, before the year is out.
This the season of unease and handball.
This where dry noodles are pooled for tourneys
In the yard, where rubber pick-pocks off brick
And toothbrush grips get real sharp, where Sharky
Dropped the forty-five-pound plate on Zed's throat,
Where Nazis plot, bleach shirts, evangelize,
Where a colon's a suitcase, a head nod
A death stroke, sightline, lifeline, where guards' wings
Are bear spray and sound like intercom fizz,
Where lights-out means scream dumb shit, where men fall
From tiers to check-in to seg, where home is
A volta that drags me back, where I nod,
Enter the cell and whisper *Here I am.*

STAGE FIVE

Incorporation of Exploitative Norms
of Prison Culture

Some of the Local Spots

Skateboarding is a poetry of motion.[14]
— Stevie Williams

THE PIZZA LEDGE

The street is finally dry
enough to skate.
For instance, we Xerox
coupons to eat for free
and waxed curbs
grind themselves down
into evening, lavender
scented candles, pockets lined
with grated sunlight.
For instance, I go shoeless
to foot race, likewise handspring.
Crushed dandelion stalks
feel lubed up and reek
of semen and honey.

MUFFIN TOPS

I'm bright for it. I run outside
to eat a peach, sugar,
sugar, sugar. A bottle rocket,
a green Bic, a new deck
with the little angel
in a silk nightie and halo
and high kick! Sometimes
I get carried away.

Sometimes I push push glide
past hall monitors,
high-vis vests gleaming
erotic light, thick
body-spray flame
in the change room dark.

THE PLAZA
Did I stutter? Did I
darkslide and ride away clean?
Take my bus pass.
I'm transferring to Love Park
to shred with Stevie Williams.
I am blind in your sun, Stevie.
I'm that ginger punk
skitching car bumpers
on a stolen board
with razor tail and a faux hawk.
I borrow your cologne.
On the house. On the school
but stealth, awning to air duct,
just tuck and roll.

McCRANK'S POOL
How long can you hold
your breath? Do you talk?
Do a dead-hang on the low dive
and I'll climb up you. Goggle this
midnight and how the streetlight
touches your braces.

You're out there and I could be fancy.
Let's lie down in the road, darling.
The sewers moan.
One plane gaps IHOP.
Feel my skateboard rattle
as I ollie over you.
If I'm moonwalking,
you're a supernova.

THE UNDERGROUND

Probly the cineplex side door
opens with a knife.
Bring flashlights and spray paint.
The abandoned parkade,
perfect for tre-flips, echoes
and sets the darkness rhyming.
I stomp it bolts, loiter, solicit boots.
Probly hand-me-down dickies
and garage moonshine
from plastic spoons. Benedryl puke,
half-naked, sweet momma
thinks it's spaghetti poison.
I used to paper bag
but now I just float.

SEVENOAKS

Maybe church but I doubt it.
If eyes closed, heads bowed,
I'm open on holidays.
The gymnasium is waxed

and I'm powersliding across galaxies.
People say dark matter or loudspeaker
but I'm here for hot buns, baby.
For instance, heavy drum solo
and show me one fence unjumpable.
The field is empty.
I'm going way downtown.
It'll be a long night so help me God,
just gimme a wet dream
and fresh grip tape.

ELISA'S BACKYARD

Shepherd me, oh Lord! oh lovely!
into your father's treehouse.
I am a scar's width
of dusted sunlight,
bright as OJ spilling
across your plywood floor.
The bottle is spinning.
I double dog dare you. I exhale
and lean on your shoulder.
You make me want to shoplift
on molly, read Keats,
pop fakie into a lens flare.
I practiced my breakdance.
Keep me out after dark.

STAGE SIX

*Diminished Sense of Self-Worth and
Personal Value*

Diesel Therapy

Five out of six inmates will be arrested within nine years
following their release. The vast majority will be arrested
within the first three.[15]

It was the same time last year, the same place,
Same white van of Plexiglas and sorrow
Idling below the ankle-chain courtroom
Where Grandma wept in the same way, silent,
Hard. And the same judge! Exactly the same
Curtain robe wherefrom the folds he unsheathed
His oversized fountain pen. What a tool,
Your honour. What girth and alacrity
With which you knick out bits of ligament
From the exposed flesh of my body clock.
Steel bunks, holding cells, bleach fumes, pizza pops,
Fingerprints, stale interrogation rooms.
The van revs. The garage doors rise. Drive me
Down that same long road. I'm yours. Take me home.

I Like to Lie Here with My Eyes Closed and Think about My Schoolfriends' Streets Before Choosing One to Walk Down Slowly, Lawn by Moonlit Lawn.

> We must live
> with the small script of the grass
> and the laughter from cellars.
> — Tomas Tranströmer

Down that same long road. I'm yours. Take me home.
I'm barefoot and flushed. Streetlamps spark the dew,
The sidewalk thrums. I'm stupidly happy.
Whiff of spring rain and asphalt. My jaw throbs
From too much molly, jabber, and hot palms
Pour themselves into bright constellations
Of grass. Each blade carbonated in-house
Inhales me, exhales pure sugar. Moonscaped
Spray-on lawns I footbath across, stainless
They say but still green-green. The cedars' black
Fingers, the timber swings, the dim laughter
Of old friends alive somewhere in the dark.
Can I stay here? Can we? Can this poem
Be more than a dream home, all talk, false hope?

Be a Man

The focus on aggressive displays, or what some describe as *hegemonic masculinity*, in part reflects the broader cultural and often patriarchal milieu in which men live out their lives prior to incarceration. The conditions are amplified under the deprivations embedded in the prison experience. The relative losses of autonomy, liberty, security, hetero-sexual relations, and basic goods and services strip away many of the core features that establish men's identities and define masculinity in the outside world.[16]

Be more than a dream home, all talk, false hope.
Be more, much more: a signpost, a springboard.
Be a big wood bowl of tropical fruit.
Be more meat and potato bread, please. More
Good Mennonite, less let's go fuck shit up.
Be a bro, man. Be tall, dark, and handsome.
Be the big bang in a single migraine.
Be bad, boy. Be nice, guy. Be suave. Be cool.
Beeline down the cul-de-sac for ice cream!
Be half knife, half nail file. Be less dad now,
More mustache dad with Ray-Bans. Be a wave
Of remorse. Be free. Be good for nothing.
A glass jar of coins. A red wheelbarrow.
A far-off storm, a rose, a dirt catwalk.

Fun and Games

The order of day-to-day prison life offers routine, and prisoners
often find their way through stressful situations over time,
and they can handle them more effectively using learned and
well-practiced reactions.[17]

A far-off storm, a rose, a dirt catwalk.
A shot called, a skull gash, a steel gangway.
A guy walks into a cell with laced shoes—
One guard says drama, one just smiles and nods—
Then walks out shirtless with two balloon hands.
Also, the funny sounds! The pay phone chime
When Tuna's forehead gets slammed into it,
Big John's back-flop, tossed from the second tier.
Preach's eyes wide at the poker table
When Psycho cracks his dome with a sock lock.
How 'bout all shirts get swastikas bleached in.
How 'bout a murder pic taped to Games' chest.
I laugh so hard my hair falls out. I die.
I laugh and laugh till Warden fears the dutch.

Old Age and Wolves

> Prison and jail telecom and commissary functions have spawned
> multi-billion dollar private industries.[18]

I laugh and laugh till Warden fears the dutch.
The dutch is a salve for old age and wolves.
Old age and wolves are frenemies on break.
Frenemies on break with new flip phones laugh
Then punch each other in the arm too hard
Behind the Sunglass Hut. The Sunglass Hut!
O, last bastion of laissez-faire markets,
Your poster is one badass dog, a pug,
The spirit animal of all poets
Since all poets are part noble, part doomed,
Doomed to daydreams, their drill tests of glass teeth
And death, death with a mouth full of red birds.
They flap and climb over one another.
Red birds staring out, plucking themselves bald.

Red Birds

Perhaps prison itself is seen as a dehumanizing institution, meaning that the longer one serves, the more one is seen as lacking humanlike capacities, becoming more like a (threatening) animal over the course of a prison sentence.[19]

Red birds staring out, plucking themselves bald.
Red birds on a spiritual retreat.
Red birds tear bibles in half then eat lunch.
Red birds huddle and laugh with hooch-red tongues.
Red birds whiff the singe of mace on raw skin.
Red birds push all-in with twelve ramen packs.
Red birds, barred meds, heed the voice of madness.
Red birds strut past cell doors, wordless and slow.
Red birds, once freed, fly off into nothing.
Red birds rust-toned with false teeth and moth breath.
Red birds still wince at key chains and flashlights.
Red birds steal steaks to return each winter.
At night they dream. They clack their beaks and flap.
In the hush all their hearts patter like rain.

Hard Time

In prison, more than 50% of those who were medicated
for mental health conditions at admission did not receive
pharmacotherapy.[20]

In the hush all their hearts patter like rain.
Or is that the clock that towers above
The chow hall? Its face behind a red flare
Ignites the polished floor. Men avoid it.
They scamper like ants around its bright beam.
The clock stalks them. It's rogue and out for blood.
The clock hikes its charred robe and taps barefoot
Past cell doors. Listen: the shadow ticking
Days on the wall is just the start. Hard time.
It drives us. It drags some straight to ding-wing.
It brings dudes to your cell before discharge
For a send-off, guards, mace, brings you to seg
Where there's new clocks: meal carts, deadbolts, wash breaks.
Cage lights on bright white walls buzzing all night.

Getting Netted Up

I was angry, lying on the butcher's
paper. My empty silhouette profane.
Coloured crayons and glitter glue ragged.
I told the intake nurse I no longer heard voices.
— Amber Dawn, *Where the words end and my body begins*

Cage lights on bright white walls buzzing all night
Are such fanatic hosts. I try to sleep
While they glow above me. It's too much glee.
It's too much beaming when I do push-ups.
I'm afraid to speak. One word and they grin
Till their tongues show. They make no sense! They're nuts
For small talk, eye contact. They clear their throats
Then push two clean jumpsuits through the food chute.
I squat on the steel shitter. They don't blink.
I strip, pace, sprawl face down. I masturbate
Till nothing but a pulse breaks the surface
Upstream from cold sweats, dread, shift change, breakfast.
The cage lights want to chat but I'm dead tired!
They smile, hum softly, lean down, thumb my cheek.

Joint Custody

Dear Daniel Scott,
who in the third grade prayed,
Lord, I want to be a fire truck,
I'm sorry your dreams have by now
burnt out.
— Kayla Czaga, *For Your Safety Please Hold On*

They smile, hum softly, lean down, thumb my cheek.
I'm the product of green shag and reruns.
I was molded out of tinfoil and glued
First to one, then to the other. Green shag
Struts around all chest hair and jorts. His do
Bobs and he gesticulates when he thinks.
He almost cracked perpetual motion
Then caught the gambling bug. The sort that digs
Into ears and whispers *Hit me, sugar.*
Reruns pulls down floral curtains to sew
Pantsuits and skirts for her trailer boutique.
She wears me on her head like antennae.
I'm here, I tell her, and move one thin arm.
Let me clear things up. I can make this work.

Learning How to Jail

They don't believe it. But for me, it was a school.
— Juvenile Inmate, unnamed[21]

Let me clear things up. I can make this work.
First, know the shoes. A cellie's boots cinched tight,
Pantlegs tucked into socks, left foot forward.
Then the room inhales you. We are all here
To smarten up. Read vibes. Note the showers,
One to cook pruno, one for shot-callers.
Which books, whose cards. Learn where to eat breakfast,
This pay phone, that chow line. Don't watch convicts
Pack suitcases, sharpen shivs in the yard.
There hasn't been a death since November.
Don't sell wolf tickets, don't dry snitch. Jumpsuits:
Part pillow, part sleep mask. When night falls, wait
Two hours. The cinderblock walls sweat. I'm here
To learn my lesson. I'm here to excel.

Fighting The Hills Have Eyes

> I remember how the darkness of the blood
> relinquished the darkness of my hands
> and snaked into the darkness of the lake.
> — Rob Taylor, *The Other Side of Ourselves*

To learn my lesson. I'm here to excel,
I tell myself and step into his room
Ten minutes till lockdown. The blue night-light
Obscures him there like blood in a dark lake.
To stand up tall. To move like fire. I'm here,
Hands held high, red head buzzed. He clips a jab
Off my ear. I whiff a left hook, clinch, slip
Back, huff into his chest, half off the bunk
As each second breaks out in warm fistfuls
Across my skull across rage across fear.
I'm here with his belly between my teeth.
To kick at the darkness. To not get pinned
In these cycles of *breathe* and *just write it*.
I'm still here, gripping my pen like a shiv.

Prison Economics

A strike by federal inmates over a cut in their pay that began in Ontario has now spread to prisons in New Brunswick, Québec, and Saskatchewan...the strikes have also forced the shutdown of the government's CORCAN operations inside the prisons. CORCAN makes textiles, furniture, and other goods for the war machine.
— Mercedes Eng, *Prison Industrial Complex Explodes*

I'm still here, gripping my pen like a shiv.
Dear Warden Voigt, your prison industry
Is one ounce of sugar sold for ten stamps
Minus Big John with steaks under each arm
From the kitchen. CO Bass hooks us up.
Really, it is more like twelve cents an hour
To unpack and rebrand machinery
Of the free market. It's all a hustle,
Prison wine in garbage bags with fruit flies
Burped down to white lightning, housemaids, bookies,
Heroin-soaked bible scraps, lip balm caps
Of Spice. Orderly Reno delivers
By hand to each cell. Dear Warden, we team
Our stock. My hands, your means. We make it work.

Afterwards, Some Place Bets on If and When He Checks In

> If you put your guard down… They see this as weakness…
> You cannot show weakness… Be strong and hold your ground
> and put your head up. Whatever comes, come.
> — Inmate, unnamed[22]

Our stock. My hands, your means. We make it work.
Old timers used to get Christmas boxes
From the local church: ramen, toiletry.
But that was scrapped. That was too much good shit.
What is this, a country club? We make do.
We brew pruno in the shower, pool stamps
Of acid, skip breakfast to wait in line
At the pay phone. One man calls his daughter
And sobs. *What did Santa bring you, honey?*
When he lays the handset in its cradle
His eyes shine with fear. Some laugh. Some look down.
Most know he won't make the new year. *I cry
Like a man*, he says and stands there, breathing
In sweet wine, cheap soap, what feels like envy.

Keep Breathing

Prisoners are vulnerable to developing mental health
problems given the significant stressors associated with
detention such as separation from family, overcrowding,
lack of privacy, boredom, poor mental stimulation, long
periods spent alone and fear of assault.[23]

In, sweet wine, cheap soap, what feels like envy.
Out, paranoia, I am, and stay out!
In, routine push-ups, dread, endless bibles.
Out of my mouth a flush of startled birds.
In, potatoes and varied hues of slop.
Outside, please, just a window, I can't breathe.
Incoming suitcase. Let's all watch him shit
Out sixty balloon pellets of cocaine.
In, all ye sinners for last man standing!
Out, but twice as old, and Lord, take me back
In where time's razor sharp at fourteen lines.
Out, worth. In, blues. Out, dead hair. In, all day
And a night. Out—wait, my hands are shaking.
Everything is going to be okay.

A Charm against Backsliding

> In the criminal justice field, the raw material is prisoners, and
> industry will do what is necessary to guarantee a steady supply.
> — Steven Donziger, *The Real War on Crime*

Everything is going to be okay.
Whenever the cell opens and its groan
Hinges on each new mistake recorded,
Stay calm and follow the revolving door.
The terms and conditions of a live wire
Include shame and hard labour for shit pay,
Bad dates, a halfway house with a dirt yard
Where bikes get matte spray paint and come and go.
Everything depends on a tin of butts,
God, kids, or who you ask. Some say structure.
Some, luck. Sometimes a white T and blue jeans
Makes me dance. Sometimes I stay in my room.
The low ceiling, same slow breath, same stillness.
It was the same time last year, the same place.

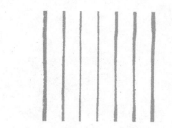

STAGE SEVEN

Post-Traumatic Stress Reactions to the
Pains of Imprisonment

The Outbreak in Mission Institution

> You can call the prison a hundred times, and no one answers.
> — Joanne Fry, mother of a sick prisoner[23]

Pacing in a concrete cell
as the virus seeps through
inmate after inmate pleading
for fresh air for vaccines
for phone calls. No chow hall
or yard time. No pencils.
Nothing sharp or breakable.
A bible. A paper suit
for any inmate caught
lashing pantlegs into rope.
The institution sequestered
like an infected zoo or warzone
or congregate setting. A closed fist
against the cold steel hatch

of hunger but I can't eat,
haven't moved my bowels
in eighteen days.
The problem sounds
like a kid screaming
there's puke everywhere
from the next cell.

The real problem
is how the night moves
around itself like blood
in the toilet.
We get twenty minutes
to stretch our legs,
shower, note who's good,

who's gone, who's curled up
in bed or mumbling
into the unit's sole pay phone
Sorry, can't hear you,
too much screaming,
I'm fine no no I'm fine,
I'll call tomorrow.
Each inmate pays
I mean prays, chants, incants
a legion of mothers
to storm the chain-link,
lines up for strip search
and headcount or files out
on a stretcher. A noose

inside a red jumpsuit.
Each night cage lights
startle into birds flocking
the epicentre of self-harm.
A white flag inside a migraine
inside a keyhole with a voice
exactly like the warden's

whispering *Right there,*
let go on three,
then a limp body
claps a plastic mattress.
A screech, a steel latch.
White noise above
fear above rage.

Good news! The face in the wall
isn't really a face,
it's a play of light.
Maybe there are layers
to this room I don't see.
A shower inside a sink.
An old window in the brickwork.
I scratch the wall paint
into thumb blood into transcript
of a prisoner whistling
to another prisoner,
then a sunbeam blinds me
through the mail slot,
or is that a flashlight?

Nights spent reading psalms,
white cinder block creased in
like one great fist,
are really a broken home
for the abandoned
protocols of embracing
one will die. Yes.

If you stopped by
to hear steel doors drum
countless shoe soles
kicking out past timelessness,
you came to the right place.
A toilet's cold bite.
A tiny wool blanket.

These evenings stay bright
as anywhere. If you stopped
by to hear the co
glide past another co
with a meal cart clicking
the world's time slot
back into place
you'll have to wait
with the rest of us.
I reach out and touch
both walls at once.
I steady myself, get dressed,
wash my neck and face.
I want to make it.

The two quotations that open this book are from, first, a speech Nelson Mandela gave after his release from prison in 1990, and second, a 2015 speech by Matthew Dickman titled "Skinheads, Suicide, and Government Assistance: Why Subjects Don't Make Poets Into Heroes."

Several of these poems first appeared in the following publications: "Forgive Me" and "Postcards from Inside the Machine" in *The Malahat Review*, "Mission" in *Geist Magazine*, "Some of the Local Spots" in *Grain Magazine*, and "The Outbreak in Mission Institution" in *Arc Poetry Magazine*.

"For This and More, I Forgive You" and "Scaring Myself" were part of a suite of poems that won runner-up in the 2020 Lush Triumphant Award and appeared in *SubTerrain Magazine*.

"Learning to Live" was shortlisted for the Hammond House International Poetry Prize and appeared in the 2022 Hammond House Anthology.

The stages comprising the seven parts of this book represent key aspects in the process of prisonization, as noted by Craig Haney in "The Psychological Impact of Incarceration: Implications for Post-Prison Adjustment."

"The Outbreak in Mission Institution" is a response to the largest prison outbreak of Covid-19 in Canada. The outbreak resulted in a segregation-like lockdown that lasted months. Inmates were released from their cell for as little as twenty minutes per day, with restrictions on any means of communication or recreation. The Correctional Service of Canada (CSC) shut down all forms of contact with the public, actively working to keep the outbreak a secret from family members and all levels of government. A coalition of distraught relatives called, emailed, and knocked on the prison doors pleading for information on their incarcerated loved ones, to no avail. Hundreds of prisoners contracted Covid-19, as well as over a dozen corrections officers. One inmate passed away from the virus.

"For This and More, I Forgive You" repurposes a line from Paul David Ashley's poem, "Prison": "If I could understand the mystery of rain / how it holds its dignity / in the violence of a storm."

"Daydreaming in the Shower before Lights-Out II" borrows from Valery Bryusov's one line poem: "Oh! Her thighs!"

"Back to Church" borrows a line from Robert Browning's poem, "Fra Lippo Lippi": "Lord, I'm not angry! Bid your hang-dogs go."

"Indigo" repurposes a line from Mary Oliver's poem, "Have you ever tried to enter the long black branches": "Listen, are you breathing just a little, and calling it a life?"

"The Day My Hair Starts to Fall Out in Clumps" and "The Season of Unease" repurpose lines from the "Shih Ching," a song of soldiers guarding the frontier: "Oh to go home, to go home / Before the year is over!"

"Some of the Local Spots" repurposes a line from Seamus Heaney's poem, "Personal Helicon": "I rhyme / To see myself, to set the darkness echoing."

"I Like to Lie Here with My Eyes Closed and Think about My Schoolfriends' Streets Before Choosing One to Walk Down Slowly, Lawn by Moonlit Lawn"; the title borrows lines from Nick Laird's titular poem, "Feel Free": "I like to lie here / with my eyes closed and think about my schoolfriends' houses before / choosing one to walk through slowly, room by sunlit room."

1 Proctor, S.L., Hoffmann, N.G., and Allison, S. (2012). "The Effectiveness of Interactive Journaling in Reducing Recidivism Among Substance-Dependent Jail Inmates." *International Journal of Offender Therapy and Comparative Criminology*, 56(2), 317–332.

2 Campbell, A. (2012). *A Place Apart: The Harm of Solitary Confinement* (Order No. MR85177). Faculty of Law, University of Toronto. Available from ProQuest Dissertations & Theses Global (1323849621).

3 Paterson-Young, C., Hazenburg, R., and Bajwa-Patel, M. (2019). *The Social Impact of Custody on Young People in the Criminal Justice System*. London: Palgrave Macmillan. Accessed at SpringerLink.

4 Dolovich, S. (2012). "Two Models of the Prison: Accidental Humanity and Hypermasculinity in the L.A. County Jail." *Journal of Criminal Law and Criminology*, 102(4), 965–1117. https://scholarlycommons.law.northwestern.edu/jclc/vol102/iss4/1.

5 McMaster, G.J. (2015). "Long-Term Solitary Segregation in the United States and Canada." In S.C. Richards (Ed.), *The Marion Experiment: Long-Term Solitary Confinement and the Supermax Movement*. Carbondale: Southern Illinois University Press.

6 Hughes, S.D. (2020). "Release Within Confinement: An Alternative Proposal for Managing the Masturbation of Incarcerated Men in U.S. Prisons." *Journal of Positive Sexuality*, 6(1), 4–23.

7 Troshynski, E.I., and Magnus, A.M. (2014). "Institutionalization." In B.A. Arrigo (Ed.), *Encyclopedia of Criminal Justice Ethics*, Vol. 1, 481–482. Los Angeles: SAGE Publications.

8 Mejia-O'Donnell, T.M. (2019). *Exploring Inmates' Prison Pen-Pal Soliciting Profiles on www.writeaprisoner.com* (Order No. 27539484). School of Public Affairs, San Diego State University. Available from ProQuest Dissertations & Theses Global (2318673665).

9 Giordano, P.C. (2010). *Legacies of Crime: A Follow-Up of the Children of Highly Delinquent Girls and Boys*. Cambridge: Cambridge University Press. https://doi.org/10.1017/CBO9780511810046.

10 Paat, Y., Hernandez, E., Hope, T.L., Muñoz, J., Zamora Jr., H., Sanchez, M.H., and Contreras, S. (2020). "'Going Solo' or Joining Gangs While Doing Time: Perceptions of Prison Gangs Among the Formerly Incarcerated." *Justice System Journal*, 41(3), 259–276.

11 Office of the Correctional Investigator of Canada. (2014). *A Three Year Review of Federal Inmate Suicides (2011–2014) Final Report*. https://www.oci-bec.gc.ca/cnt/rpt/oth-aut/oth-aut20140910-eng.aspx.

12 Kim, C.Y., Losen, D.J., and Hewitt, D.T., (2010). *The School-to-Prison Pipeline: Structuring Legal Reform.* New York: New York University Press. Accessed at Project MUSE: https://muse.jhu.edu/book/11120.

13 Guenther, L. (2013). *Solitary Confinement: Social Death and Its Afterlives.* Minneapolis: University of Minnesota Press. Accessed at Project MUSE: https://muse.jhu.edu/book/26792.

14 Brinkworth, A. (2020). "Poetry of Motion–The Timber Skate Bowl." Building Centre, August 4, 2020. https://www.buildingcentre.co.uk/news/articles/poetry-of-motion-the-timber-skate-bowl.

15 Alper, M., and Durose, M.R. (2018). 2018 *Update on Prisoner Recidivism: A 9-Year Follow-up Period (2005-2014).* Special Report, Bureau of Justice Statistics, U.S. Department of Justice. https://bjs.ojp.gov/content/pub/pdf/18upr9yfup0514.pdf.

16 Michalski, J.H. (2019). "The Challenge of Redefining the Imprisoned Self as an Artist: The Pedagogical Rituals of a Prison Arts Instructor." *Howard Journal of Crime and Justice*, 58(1), 65–85.

17 Kovács, Z., Kun, B., Griffiths, M.D., and Demetrovi, Z. (2019). "A Longitudinal Study of Adaption to Prison After Initial Incarceration." *Psychiatry Research*, 273, 240–246.

18 Sawyer, W., and Wagner, P. (2023). "Mass Incarceration: The Whole Pie 2023." Prison Policy Initiative press release, March 14, 2023. https://www.prisonpolicy.org/reports/pie2023.html.

19 Deska, J.C., Almaraz, S.M., and Hugenberg, K. (2020). "Dehumanizing Prisoners: Remaining Sentence Duration Predicts the Ascription of Mind to Prisoners." *Personality and Social Psychology Bulletin*, 46(11), 1614–1627. https://doi.org/10.1177/0146167220911496.

20 Reingle Gonzalez, J.M., and Connell, N.M. (2014). "Mental Health of Prisoners: Identifying Barriers to Mental Health Treatment and Medication Continuity." *American Journal of Public Health,* 104(12), 2328–2333.

21 Zoetti, P.A. (2015). "My Body Imprisoned, My Soul Relieved: Youth, Gangs and Prison in Cape Verde." *European Journal of Cultural Studies*, 21(2), 148–164.

22 Fraser, A. (2009). "Mental Health in Prisons: A Public Health Agenda." *International Journal of Prisoner Health,* 5(3), 132–140. https://doi.org/10.1080/17449200903115789.

23 Penner, P. (2020). "Mission Institution: Voices from Inside Canada's Worst COVID-19 Prison Outbreak." *Abbotsford News*, April 30, 2020. https://www.abbynews.com/news/mission-institution-voices-from-inside-canadas-worst-covid-19-prison-outbreak/.

GLOSSARY

AIN'T RIGHT: A violent inmate of questionable sanity who should be avoided.

ALL DAY AND A NIGHT: Life without parole.

BAM-BAM: A mentally ill inmate, often one who is erratic or violent.

BEAN SLOT: Door slot through which food trays are inserted. Also, slot through which seg prisoners are cuffed prior to leaving their cell.

BLUES: Prison issued clothes. Depending on the prison and colour, can also be "Reds."

BOBOS: Prison issued shoes, usually white canvas Velcro sneakers.

BOUNCED: When someone is attacked with the sole intention of getting them off the unit.

THE BOX: Segregation or solitary confinement. A small, windowless, perpetually lit cell where an inmate is only allowed out for one twenty-minute shower break each day.

CHATTED OUT: Someone who has lost their mind while in prison.

CHECK IN: To enter segregation voluntarily, usually for fear of one's safety on a specific unit.

CHRIST AIR: A skateboard trick where a skater launches into the air, grabs the board with one hand, and spreads their arms.

COS: Corrections Officers.

CONVICT: An experienced, professional inmate.

DIESEL THERAPY: An unspoken form of punishment where prisoners are shackled and then transported for an entire day, days, or weeks.

DING-WING: The mental health ward.

DRAMA: A fight or an assault.

DRY SNITCH: To snitch indirectly by talking loudly or drawing attention.

(DO) THE DUTCH: To commit suicide.

FISH: New, first-time inmates; someone who appears naive and vulnerable.

FOOD CHUTE: Door slot (see bean slot).

GONZO: An inmate who is off their meds.

HARD TIME: Serving a long prison sentence. Also, time served in the hole.

HILL BOMB: Skateboarding downhill at high speeds without stopping.

THE HOLE: Segregation (see The Box).

HOUSEMAID: Someone who cleans other inmates' cells, either for stamps or commissary, or for protection.

(TO) JAIL: To be knowledgeable about, and to follow the rules or etiquette set by the prisoners.

J-BUG: A prisoner who needs mental health treatment.

LACED UP: Cinching the Velcro of one's shoes; a sign meaning that person is planning to fight.

MONKEY MOUTH: An individual who won't stop talking. Often associated with mental illness.

NETTED UP: An inmate who experiences a mental breakdown in prison.

NEWSPAPER SHANK: A quick and simple shank made out of paper hardened and molded in layers with toothpaste and water.

PAPER SUIT: A prison jumpsuit made of paper issued to inmates who are on suicide watch, usually accompanied by a loss of bedding and toiletries, often taking place in segregation.

POWERSLIDE: Turning the skateboard sideways, suddenly, and at high speed so the wheels drift across the floor.

PRUNO: Prison wine. Alcohol made from various fruit juice, fruit, fruit peels, and bread mixed in a garbage bag and left to ferment.

PSYCH CAMP: The mental health ward.

RAZOR TAIL: When a skateboard is so old the tail has been worn down to a short, sharp edge.

RED SCORPIONS: A violent gang formed in 2010, based in the Fraser Valley of British Columbia, Canada.

RED TAG: To be confined to one's cell as a disciplinary measure.

SEG: Segregation (see The Box).

SHOT CALLER: A prominent gangster on a unit who has the authority to tell people what to do, and to direct violence.

SKID BID: A short jail stint or prison sentence.

SKITCH: To hold the bumper of a moving car while on a skateboard.

SLEEP ON STEEL: Having your mattress, sheets, and blanket taken away. Can be a form of punishment, or due to being a suicide risk.

SOCK LOCK: A pad lock or similar small, hard object placed in a sock. A common prison weapon.

SPICE: A strong synthetic cannabinoid made from organic materials such as herbs coated in household chemicals. When smoked, you temporarily enter a zombie-like, unresponsive stupor.

STAMPS: Mail stamps, a common prison currency.

STOMP IT BOLTS: To land a trick perfectly and with style.

SUITCASE: One's rectum, used to conceal contraband.

TORPEDO: An enforcer. Someone eager to follow the orders of the shot caller in order to earn credibility and respect.

TURTLE SUIT: A padded anti-suicide smock worn by inmates at risk of self-harm.

UNDER WATCH: An inmate, often with mental health problems, who is confined to their cell.

VAMPIRE: Someone who draws blood. Can either mean in a fight, or from cutting themselves.

WHITE LIGHTNING: A high proof moonshine made from distilled prison wine.

WOBBLE HEAD: Prisoner with mental health issues or on medication.

WOLF TICKETS: To talk tough without intending to back it up.

WOLVES: Inmates who are normally straight on "the outside" but engage in sexual activity with men while incarcerated.

X-CAT: A lifer or long-term inmate in need of mental health evaluation.

ACKNOWLEDGMENTS

My deepest gratitude to the following:

Rob Taylor, for introducing me to poetry, and for your early and ongoing encouragement.

Sheryda Warrener, for your invaluable guidance and inspiration. This book wouldn't exist without you.

Nick Thran, for being a thoughtful and meticulous editor, and for championing my manuscript.

Amy Chiasson, for always being a great listener, and for believing in me.

My family, for your unwavering love and support.

And Brick Books, for taking a chance and supporting this work.

BRADLEY PETERS grew up in the Fraser Valley, BC, graduated from UBC's Creative Writing Program, and has since been shortlisted or named runner-up for numerous awards. In 2019, Bradley won the annual Short Grain Contest, and his poems have appeared in *Arc, Geist, Grain, SubTerrain, The Malahat Review*, and elsewhere. This is his debut poetry collection. He lives in Chilliwack, where he works as an actor and carpenter.

Achevé d'imprimer
sur les presses de l'imprimerie Gauvin,
Gatineau, Québec, Canada